'New Life Rising' (detail),
Leslie Morgan

'Fragments of Survival',
Leslie Morgan

'Contrasting States' (detail),
Claire Benn

Preface

Both of us love 'wet work'; the act of using dyes, discharge media, textile paints and metal leaf to create cloth that is multi-layered and rich in depth. The possibilities seem never-ending and the more we explore, the more exciting the journey becomes.

We would exhort you to be willing to have a go, play and practice just for the sake of finding out what can happen. At the same time, you'll be producing cloth that's based on your experiments and samples, your subsequent observations, your modifications, your choices – truly your own, personal cloth.

How you then use that cloth is up to you. Leslie is a quilt maker who loves to piece in a free, improvisational and spontaneous way. She cuts up her cloth and sews it back together again with new room-mates, or in different configurations. Claire tends to work with whole cloth. If the piece works as 'art cloth' or 'complex cloth' it's left to be art in it's own right, free-hanging or sometimes stretched or mounted on to canvas. Other pieces may be stitched, quilted, used for soft furnishing items such as cushions and throws, or used as yardage for clothing. The use of cloth is almost unlimited.

In our experience, people fear the (silk) screen. This is perhaps due to its history and use in precise registration printing. But it doesn't have to be like that. Using a screen can be a free and spontaneous affair and this book aims to introduce you to one of the many approaches it has to offer.

Simply put, 'breakdown' printing involves applying thick dye paints or print paste directly on to the back of the screen. This is left to dry and then printed off with more dye paint or print paste, or a combination thereof. This print 'media' (the dye) is gradually dissolving the dried-on dye on the screen – it's breaking down and printing an ever-changing array of colours, marks, textures and distressed, organic and disintegrating effects.

This is not a process for those who are oriented to the precise! Whilst, with practice, the process is controllable, one of its joys is never quite knowing how quickly things will happen and how – exactly – the imagery and textures may change.

So, we encourage you to give it a go and embark on your own journey.

'Pressure Point' (detail),
Claire Benn

Using This Book

This is not a comprehensive guide to every option available to you when screen printing. However, we have provided some background information about the (silk) screen itself, setting up your workspace and general printing tips and techniques. For a detailed guide to a greater range of screen printing approaches, we recommend Jane Dunnewold's book 'Improvisational Screen Printing' (self published, see the 'Further Reading' section).

There is only one rule for this process; only use dye paints or clear, thick chemical paste/print paste on the screen. Do not use screen inks – if left to dry on the screen, they will seal the mesh forever and render the screen useless!

The first printing approach in the 'Get Going' section covers 'Making an Impression' and also explains the general technique of using dye-on-screen. The other variables will refer you back to this section as we wanted to avoid repetition and once you've had a couple of goes, we're confident you'll get the hang of it!

In the beginning, work at samples – don't lay down a 2 metre length of fabric and go at it. With a standard size (30x44cm) screen, 50-75cm lengths are more than adequate. In fact, a standard screen won't go the distance with this particular approach on large pieces of cloth; you'll either need a larger screen, or several screens at once. Worry about that once you've understood the key principles and made some discoveries of your own.

Buying a book is one thing. Implementing what's in it is another. Different things drive different people, and the way we approach learning anything new can vary enormously from one individual to another. A theory exists from educationalist Peter Honey that poses four different learning 'styles'. We've taken a light-hearted twist on it below, so see if you can recognise yourself...

- *Activists*; look at the pictures, get excited, skim the text and jump right in.

- *Reflectors*; mull over what they've seen and read, stroke the pictures, daydream about the possibilities, start eventually.

- *Theorists*; read the book from cover to cover, decide on a logical place to start (which isn't necessarily where we recommend), write their own list of what to do, double check everything and then start.

- *Pragmatists*; consider if the contents are of any use to their discipline and speculate as to whether it really is a process that can be done in the kitchen. If the end result seems to have potential, they'll give it a go.

Left: Christine & Mary exploring 'Breakdown Printing' in the Committed to Cloth studio

Some people have a very dominant style. Others might have a preference for two styles. Some may even be fairly balanced across all four. It doesn't matter what your style is, just get started somehow, sometime!

Nothing contained in this book is meant to be restrictive or set in concrete. Every time we use this particular screen printing process, we discover something new and exciting or think of other ways of going at it. A key question to constantly ask is "what if?" Experimentation, combining approaches and practice, practice, practice will enable you to make discoveries and create some great cloth. And remember, to get really good cloth generally takes at least three processes (often more) and you can combine different processes to achieve that 'Complex Cloth' look (Jane Dunnewold, Fibre Studio Press, 1996). Experiment and work at it and you'll get cloth that works for you.

The key thing is not to be intimidated. Be inspired; "every journey begins with a single step". Keep an open mind, manage your expectations, do everything at least three times, keep asking 'what if' and enjoy the journey.

The work of an Activist!

Silk Habotai, breakdown printed, then discharged printed using a thermofax screen

The Work Area

Wet work can be done in the kitchen, a garage, a garden shed or even out in the garden. Whilst a wet studio is the ideal, we both started under kitchen/garden conditions.

However, setting up the work area is important. If possible, use an area with washable surfaces, or plan to lay down heavy plastic sheeting. Worrying about drips and spills will distract you from the work in hand. You'll also need an area for wash-up of tools. Whilst a kitchen sink isn't quite big enough to hold a 30x44cm silkscreen, it's still possible to wash one up without it being laid flat. A reasonable alternative is a large plastic box that you can park outside near a drain and fill with water from a hose. Place the box on a small picnic table to help your back rather than squatting at ground level.

Printing Surfaces / Workbenches

Generally speaking, if you have to bend too much when painting or printing your back will complain, so try and work at a table height that's slightly below waist height (kitchen worktop height – between 85-95 cm). You can raise your kitchen table on bricks or wooden blocks, and keep these stored in the garden/garage/shed/ understairs cupboard.

Our workbenches/printing boards are made from 12mm MDF or Plywood and can be cut to any size. They have then been covered by stretching and stapling two layers of acrylic felt over them. Two layers of old blanket or even a layer of old-fashioned carpet underlay is also a good option, but either way, avoid a consistency that's too soft/spongy. Stockists of wide acrylic felt are shown under the supplier list. The print board can be stored behind a wardrobe, under a bed or in the garage/shed – so with a bit of effort, any kitchen can be turned into a studio for a day – and worst case scenario means waiting for a fine day and working in the garden.

For this process (and it's generally true for most screen-printing processes) we cover the bench with a drop-cloth; cotton loomstate, calico or an old bed sheet are all good options. The drop cloth absorbs excess media and prevents bleeding. Some of ours have become so magnificent they've been withdrawn from service and turned into storage bags for our work.

Media

Recipes for making up Chemical Water, Chemical/Print Paste and dye paints are at the back of the book, as is a resources list.

- Procion Mx dyes; as a minimum colour range we recommend having dyes in Scarlet Red Mx-3G, Magenta Red Mx-8B, Bright Turquoise Mx-G, Royal Blue Mx-R, Acid Lemon Mx-8G and Golden Yellow Mx-3R. We source from Kemtex and these are the names they use. You can mix any colour from these six basic primaries. However, feel free to invest in a larger colour range – we do! Other good Kemtex Procion Mx colours include Kenactive Black K2647, Indigo Navy Mx-2G, Red-Brown Mx-5BR, Dark Brown Mx-3G and Olive Green Mx-G. We also tend to stock Charcoal, Rust Orange and Petrol Green from their 'CD' range.

- Urea; a hydroscopic agent (it constantly attracts moisture from the air) and keeps the dye paint from drying out too quickly.

- Water softener (such as Calgon); using a water softener is important if you live in a hard water zone.

- Ludigol/Resist Salt L (optional); this is an anti-oxidant that helps to keep the dye colours bright in areas of high pollution. It's an optional extra and very small quantities are needed.

- Manutex/Sodium Alginate; the thickening agent for making Print Paste from the Chemical Water. Dye is then added to this print paste to create a thick dye paint.

- Discharge paste; although you can make your own discharge paste, it's a hazardous and messy process. Instead, use commercially made discharge paste from Jacquard (see Resources list at rear).

These supplies would probably just about all fit into a large plastic box with a lid, such as sold in DIY shops, petrol stations or garden centres.

Tools you'll need

- screens, ideally at least 3, scrubbed, water-proofed and ready to go
- a squeegee (ideally the 9"/23cm Speedball variety)
- a selection of foam brushes
- plastic containers (with lids) for storing chemical water, print paste and mixed dyes
- a couple of cat litter trays
- 2" wide masking tape
- squeeze bottles (purpose bought or adapt household bottles)
- a box of bits such as bubble wrap, old washers, nails, corrugated card/plastic, plastic mesh, string etc.
- a drop cloth for covering the print board (in time, this will become a work of art in its own right!)
- sturdy sheet plastic, two lengths measuring 2mx1m (store rolled, not folded)
- mixing containers such as old yoghurt pots
- spoons
- rubber gloves

The Screen – General Information & use

The term silk screen printing comes from the time when the frame was stretched with a silk fabric, but now the mesh is made from polyester. Both wooden and aluminium frames are available. Aluminium is very light but replacing the mesh is almost impossible to do in a domestic studio, meaning that the frame would need to be sent back to the manufacturer. A wooden frame however, is easy to re-mesh using a staple gun.

Screen Mesh & Frames

Polyester mesh come in various types, but the one that's applicable for use with water-based products such as dye paints and discharge paste is a multi-filament mesh. It's woven from threads that have been twisted together before being woven. These strands have more "grab" than a mesh made from monofilament and get hold of water based products such as dye paints more effectively. A wide variety of mesh is available but for general-purpose a 43T (USA=10xx) mesh is most common. 43 represents the count per centimetre and the T denotes the thickness of thread in the mesh.

The mesh is stretched tightly over a wooden frame – either by stapling or glueing. Frames that have been professionally stretched usually have a better, tighter stretch than self-stretched ones, but if you do ruin a screen, you can get a reasonable stretch yourself. Suppliers of screen mesh are listed at the back of the book and guidance on how to re-mesh can be found in 'Improvisational Screen Printing' by Jane Dunnewold.

Frames come in variety of sizes, but a useful, easily manageable and easily obtainable size is 30cm x 44cm (measured from the outside edges of the screen). This gives an approximate printable area of 19cm x 33cm. You can order frames to any size, but the bigger they get, the harder they are to handle by yourself.

There are several things that will ruin/destroy a screen;

- screen inks or textile paints that have been allowed to dry on the mesh; this is why this particular process is only suitable for dye paints and print paste;

- use of inappropriate ink/paints, non-textile or quick-drying acrylic paints/inks, or mixed inks of different types or from different manufacturers that may not like each other and cause an adverse reaction on the mesh, and possibly to the cloth;

- sharp objects that may pierce or cut the mesh.

Left: Breakdown using black & rust orange dyes

Pre-Cleaning

Whether you buy pre-stretched screens or stretch them yourself, always clean them as a first step. Simply put the frame under running warm water and scrub the mesh on both sides with a cream cleanser, then rinse thoroughly. Dishwashing soap or other cleaners with an oily base are not good for cleaning as they can coat the mesh with a residue. Let the screen – and its wooden frame - dry completely before water-proofing.

Water-Proofing

The screen frame needs to be water-proofed before use as the (usually soft) wood will become saturated and potentially warp over time. Proofing screens also means that they can be wiped dry and used again within 10 minutes or so – important if you only have a limited number of screens to use.

The frame can be covered with gaffer/water-proof tape, although brands other than Duck or 3M have a tendency to lift in the UK climate. In an ideal world, give the frame three coats of water-based acrylic varnish – you'll only have to do it once! To varnish, use a water-based acrylic varnish in satin or gloss – it doesn't need to look pretty or perfect. When you varnish, be careful not to drip varnish onto the mesh as it'll block the screen. If you do, quickly wipe off the drip with a damp cloth before it has a chance to set. If you have a real disaster, use 'thinners' and a Q-Tip/rag to rub off the varnish, then wipe down the area with soapy water.

Creating the well

A selection of squeegees

Pinning out the dry, soda-soaked cloth

Creating the 'Well'

You will need to create a 'well' all around the perimeter of the screen (about 2cm wide) for the dye/ink to sit in before printing. This is easily done by using masking tape on the back of the screen. This 'well' will need to be replaced each time you use the screen as the tape usually lifts off on washing. If you ever need to tape up a part of the screen you don't want to print through, use masking tape as this makes a strong, but temporary hold. Masking tape can bond permanently if left on for very long periods of time, so be aware that a 'temporary hold' can change to a permanent one.

The Squeegee

The squeegee is the tool used to pull the media (e.g. dye, discharge paste) across the surface of the screen. The best are 9"/23cm blades from Speedball as they are made with a plastic handle and have a rounded-edge rubber blade that's light, easy to hold and easy to clean. A wooden squeegee with a thick rubber blade is harder to hold and harder to use. If you're using small frames, a grouting tool makes a pretty good squeegee. If the squeegee is significantly smaller than the silkscreen, you'll need to do more than one pull.

It's very important to try and develop good technique. Whilst there may be occasions where poor technique may yield interesting results (and 'Breakdown' printing is one of them), good technique is important as it builds confidence and is there when you need it.

Pinning Down the Cloth

When using 'Breakdown' printing, we generally don't iron the cloth we work on as we like the added texture some overall wrinkling can give, but we do iron out sharp crease lines caused by folding before pinning out.

When you print, the media will go through the prepared screen and on to the cloth, making it wet. When you pick the screen up, the cloth will try to hang on to the screen, so pinning down the cloth is important. Lay out the cloth and send ball-headed pins through the drop-cloth and into the padded surface. Push the pin right up to it's ball-head as then you'll be able to place a screen on top safely. Put the cloth under some tension as you pin as it will stretch as it gets wetter and wetter.

Laying down a 'bead' of media (in this case, discharge paste)

First pull - keep the squeegee just off the vertical

Try to remember to print off the edge of the cloth

Printing Tips & Techniques

- Position your squeegee in the well – at the top of the frame if pulling towards you, at the right of the frame if you're right-handed, at the left if you're left-handed. *Pulling the squeegee towards you, or from right to left (if right-handed) is the best way to achieve a smooth, even pull… and practice helps too.*

- Having positioned your squeegee, spoon/pour the chosen media into the 'well' in a line in front of the positioned squeegee – this is called a *bead.*

- Keep the handle of the squeegee just off the vertical as you pull. Try not to lean it towards you too much as close to upright generates a good print. When you get to the other end of the screen, don't push the squeegee back in the opposite direction. Instead, ease up the pressure and scoop the unused media up the side of the frame and onto the squeegee so you can deposit it back at the top/right hand side of the screen/into the well for continued printing.

- How many pulls you need will depend on your own physical strength and the fabric you're using; a fine silk will often only need one pull, with fairly light pressure. A heavy cotton may need more pulls with harder pressure. It takes practice to get your print as you want it. As you print, add more media as necessary.

- The quality of print you get is determined by (a combination of):
  - the fabric type; fine weights (such as silk Habotai 8), medium weights (such as cotton, silk-cotton), heavy weights (such as velvet, felt, heavy cottons/linen)
  - the pressure you exert; how hard you press down as you pull will affect the amount of media being deposited.
  - the media; the consistency of the media will have an impact; very thick dye paints may require more pressure, but too watery a consistency will result in bleed and run-off.
  - the number of pulls; generally speaking, between one & three pulls will be sufficient.

Ultimately, you need to practice on different fabric types and with different media to understand the effects you can get.

If you place the screen onto a printed area that's still wet, you'll pick up media on the back of the screen which will lay down a "ghost". This can give you added texture or create a mess – it depends on what you're trying to achieve. For the Breakdown process, don't worry about ghosting – it'll all add to the glorious texture!

Generally, whenever you're screen printing across the whole piece of cloth (as opposed to laying down a single, focal-point print), try to remember to print off the edge of the cloth to avoid a 'frame' around the edge.

Ultimately, practice and experimentation is the only route forward and there'll be times when you break all known rules, but start by trying to develop good print habits!

Get Going!

Preparing the Cloth

The dyes used for this process are Procion Mx fibre-reactive dyes. We source our dyes from Kemtex and the colours we refer to are Kemtex names at the time of going to print.

Procion dyes are suitable for use with natural fibres; cotton, linen, silk, viscose (rayon/cellulose) or blends thereof. Recipes for making up the dye paints are contained at the back of the book (see 'Recipes'). They require soda as a fixative which we put into the cloth rather than the dyes, as dyes with soda in them have a very limited shelf life which isn't conducive to this 'Breakdown' approach.

Washing/Scouring The Cloth

Whilst some cloth is supplied 'PDF' (meaning it's prepared for dyeing), others may not be, particularly if bought from retailers or from market stalls etc. It's important that any fabric you use is pre-washed to remove size as it can prevent the dyes from penetrating the fibres. The easiest method is to simply pre-wash your fabric at 60° C. Consider washing it twice if you feel it may have a lot of size in it.

To guarantee removal of size, it helps to scour fabric in Synthrapol SP/Metapex 38 (a rinsing agent) and soda ash. Synthrapol is a specialist washing agent used by dyers. It can be used to remove size from fabric or remove excess dye from fabric. Excess dye wants to bond with the fibres, and Synthrapol SP has been especially formulated to penetrate fibres, remove size and/or catch up and hold excess dye.

Soda ash is not household soda. Its proper name is Sodium Carbonate and it can be obtained in 5-litre + containers from swimming pool supply companies (sold as Alkali ph Plus). Be careful you don't buy a brand that has chlorine added to the soda, as this will generate disastrous results – check with the supplier that it's pure soda ash. Kemtex sell mail order in bulk and you can obtain smaller quantities from other suppliers listed under the 'Resources' section. Be careful when using soda ash; if inhaled, the fine particles are bad for the lungs, so wear a mask when measuring significant quantities.

For scouring with Synthrapol and Soda Ash, wash the fabric as follows:

- Load fabric into washing machine (don't over-fill)
- Sprinkle in 3 tablespoons of Soda Ash and a 1/2 teaspoon of Synthrapol for a full load of fabric (about 6 metres). The amount depends on the type of fabric – a fine silk will need less soda and Synthrapol than a heavy-weight cotton or velvet.
- Wash at 60° C.
- Any shrinkage will also occur at this stage, which is useful.

Left: Silk Habotai, multiple breakdown printed, discharged and over-dyed

Soda-soaking for dye paints

When printing, dyeing or painting with Procion MX dyes in this method, the fixative for the dyes (soda ash) is placed in the fabric rather than the dye.

- The soda solution will handle lots of fabric, but the exact amount is difficult to specify as it depends on the fibre. A quantity of soda solution will prepare a great deal more fine silk than it will heavy cotton, as silk fibres are finer than cotton or velvet and absorb less of the solution.

- As a general principle, for medium to heavier weight fabrics such as cotton, linen, silk/viscose velvet, cotton velvet or silk/cotton and silk/linen mixes, use 45 ml / 3 tablespoons of soda ash per litre of water, and work to about 1 litre of soda solution for between one and two metres of fabric (see recipe page 30). Again, wear a mask when mixing significant quantities of soda solution.

- Soak for 10-20 minutes in the Soda Mixture, and then either drip-dry or spin first. If you have a stand-alone spin-dryer, collect the run-off soda solution and re-use it.

- The cloth is best line-dried rather than tumble-dried for several reasons; the soda/heat combination may damage the fabric; soda can be released into the air as fine particle dust (bad for you) and a residue of soda can also be left on the drum of the tumble dryer – unpleasant and unhealthy if your bath towels go in next!

- Soda-soaked fabric can be stored for later use, but must be bone-dry. Silk will store for about a month whilst cotton, linen or viscose can be kept indefinitely.

- We don't store our soda-soaked cloth folded as the crease marks show up once printed. Instead, we scrumple it all up into a large plastic box. Equally, we generally don't iron the cloth before use – particularly with this process – as any scrumple marks are a great addition to texture.

So, your cloth is ready to go. Let's now tackle preparing the screen(s). The first approach – Making an Impression – covered in this section details the general technique of using dyes on-screen. 'Writing, Doodles & Squiggles' and 'Drips & Runs' use similar techniques. We've chosen not to repeat ourselves under each approach as once you've had a couple of goes, we're confident you'll get the hang of it! If you need to, refer back to the detail contained under 'Making an Impression'.

Before you start think about colour theory. To begin, it can be helpful to work in a range of two primaries or close colours, for example;

- *Lemon Yellow, Golden Yellow, Turquoise and Royal Blue* will give a great variety of green in addition to the individual primaries

- *Lemon Yellow, Golden Yellow, Scarlet, Magenta and Red Brown* will give you these individual colours, plus orange, ochre and 'double red'

- *Turquoise, Royal Blue, Indigo, Magenta and Scarlet* will give you the individual colours, and a range or purple, plum and aubergine.

Get ready

Squirting on the dyes prior to spreading them out

Spreading out the dyes

Making an Impression

This approach uses thick dye paints applied in a large or small range of colours. The dyes are applied directly to the back of the screen, items (such as bubble wrap) are pressed into the wet dye and the screen is then left to dry before use.

One key point to remember is that once you get to the actual print stage, the media you use to print with will dissolve these dried-on dye colours. They will mingle as you print, so if you've originally painted the screen with three primary colours, expect the print paste to potentially tint to some kind of a brown (the exact tint will be determined by the colours you've used, and their proportions).

Get Ready

Assemble the following;

- masking tape (2" wide)
- a screen (or perhaps 2)
- items to make impressions with; bubble wrap, mesh, string, washers, nails, hooks, corrugated card/plastic etc. – anything that makes an impression when pressed into the wet dye paint
- cat litter tray
- thick dye paints in your choice of colours (see 'Recipes' section at rear)
- foam brushes equivalent to the number of dye colours
- a piece of sturdy plastic, newspaper or a drop cloth
- rubber gloves

If you need/want to, create a well by using masking tape (torn or straight edge) on the back of the screen. We often don't bother creating a well – this is an organic process, so who cares about bleed.

Paint on the Dye

- Take your screen and place it so the back of the screen is facing up (e.g. the flat side is face up).

- Squirt out some dye on to the back of the screen and use a foam brush to spread it out across the mesh. It's fine if the dye layer is thicker in some areas than others – in fact, this is desirable.

- Work in sections, using a different foam brush for each colour applied. This may seem a little control-freakish, but when you print, the colours are going to mingle, so start by keeping the colours as pure as possible (but don't get stressed about it!).

Making impressions with bubble wrap and rubber mesh

Making an all-over impression with bubble wrap

Peeling off the items used to make impressions

Making Impressions

- Now press a selection (or limited range) of your assembled items on to the dye-covered screen. Press them down well so they make contact with the wet dye and leave them there until the dye is dry, or virtually dry. If these items are removed too quickly, the dye is likely to simply settle back into a smooth (ish) layer. How many items you 'make an impression' with is up to you; sometimes we use a single layer of bubble wrap, or perhaps a selection of plastic mesh. At other times we may mix the items; a piece or two of bubble wrap, some nails, some washers, a few hooks. The choice is yours and the more you experiment, the more you'll discover and the more you'll understand your own preferences for the marks made.
- Remember - you can paint up several screens at once.
- Leave the screen flat and let it dry completely – we try to place the screen somewhere warm'ish to speed up this process, so it's a great fine-weather thing to do.
- You can use a hairdryer to speed up the drying process in inclement weather, but this is very tedious as it tends to take a long time. We often bring our prepared screens into the house; place them on plastic or a drop cloth to catch the drips and leave them to dry naturally and in their own time.
- Painted-up screens can be left for about 2 weeks and still work very well, although the atmospheric conditions may affect things in terms of them staying dry or becoming damp again.
- When the dye paint is almost dry, peel off any materials that were used to make impressions and leave the screen to dry out fully. Things made of plastic can be washed and re-used, or left un-washed and re-used.

Printing Off

- Pin out your dry soda-soaked cloth on to the bench – work with un-dyed cloth or a pale pre-dyed cloth – and tension out the cloth as you pin.
- Gather together the things you'll need;

- clear print paste in a pot with a spoon, or in a squeeze bottle
- thick dye paints in your choice of colours
- a squeegee
- a cat litter tray
- rubber gloves

- Lay the screen (flat/painted side down) on to the pinned-out cloth. We recommend you don't start dead centre, or way off in a tight corner.
- Spoon or squirt some clear print paste into the top or right-hand side of the screen- you'll need a fair amount at this stage as it'll take some effort to get the dried-on dyes on the back of the screen to 'let go'.
- Pull! It's impossible to say how many pulls you'll need to get things moving as much will depend on your personal strength/technique. However, as a rough guide, it'll be somewhere between 3 and 6.
- To check if the dried-on dye paints are starting to dissolve and release, scoop out the excess media/gloop and deposit it and the squeegee in the cat litter tray. Then, anchor the screen firmly at one end and lift up the other end – take a peek and see what's happening. If there's little dye release, lay the screen flat again, scoop the gloop out of the litter tray, back into the

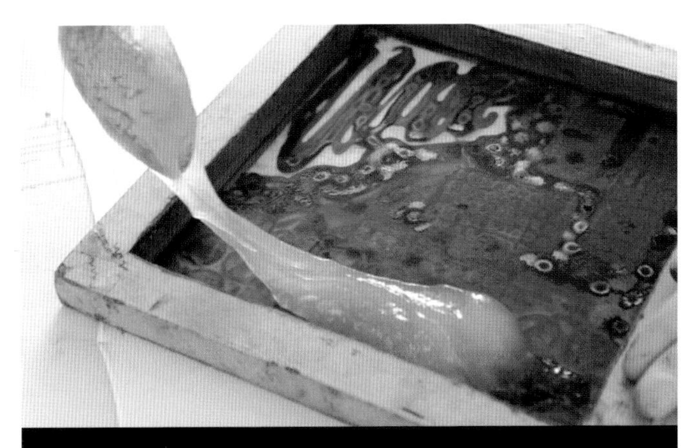

A fat bead of print paste

See how the prints become more definite

Breakdown has happened - look at how voids have been created

well and keep pulling. If you're happy with the print (and it could be quite faint at this stage), lift up the screen and re-position it.

- The 'impression' marks made by the items you stuck on should be printing off on to the cloth.
- Continue in this manner and as you print, the print paste will become tinted with the dyes from the screen, allowing you to lay down washes of colour.
- It's hard to explain exactly what will happen (remember, we said this wasn't a process for the precise!) as the dried-on dyes will print off at different speeds and saturation. This is interesting as;

- the thicker areas may be laying down very uneven areas of colour or be resisting printing – don't worry about this – treat it as a chemical resist and part of the disintegrating, organic patterning process. You often get a faint 'halo' of an edge, which is fantastic and marvellously delicate.
- you'll have outlines, texture and marks made by the impressions of the dried-on dye paint
- as the screen breaks down less dye will be left on it and organic areas of 'void' will be appearing in your prints.
- the tinted print paste will be able to get through the areas of void easily, laying down sheer washes of colour achieved through the mingling of the print paste and the dye colours on the screen.

- So, the key thing here is that the dried-on dye on the back of the screen is being dissolved by the dye you're printing with and will be breaking down. At this stage you can experiment;

- *Continue with print paste*; this will lay down very sheer/pale washes of colour through the voids as there'll be less dye on-screen to tint the print paste. You can also over-print using this method.
- *Switch to using 'standard strength' dye paints*; this will lay down darker value areas through the voids, and you can also over-print with stronger dyes. But… remember that if you started the process with print paste, the original tints and colours will be of a fairly pale strength in value terms as the print paste will have diluted the strength of the dyes on-screen. So, be aware that over-printing with a strong dye value may obscure what you've already got.
- *Switch to using diluted dye strengths*; this is a good way to start as you're less likely to obscure exiting prints when over-printing. You can decant your original dye colours into a small pot and reduce their strength (say, by half) by adding an equal amount of print paste. Or, a more organic approach is to spoon/squirt down a bead of print paste, and then add a bead of standard-strength dye paint on top of it.

- You're also free to "mix 'n match" with new colours once you've switched to using dye paints – just be aware of the possibility for mud!
- Be aware of what's happening as you work. Be careful not to over saturate the cloth with heavy handed over-printing as some of the fine, delicate textural marks/ impressions may get too wet and bleed and blur out (this can be a planned outcome, but more of this later).
- Finally, there's nothing to stop you using full or weakened dye paints from the very beginning. Decision, decisions, decisions! Just experiment!

Making suiggle marks with dye paints straight from the squeeze bottle

Writing with dye paints using a squeeze bottle

Leave the screen to dry flat

Curing & Batching

The full details of curing/batching and rinsing are covered at the back of the book as we wanted to avoid repetition in every 'variable' of the process. However, the key things to bear in mind are;

- cloth with dye-paint applications need moisture (a lot or a little), heat (between 15-35°C) and time (a minimum of 4 hours, ideally 12-18 hours, e.g. overnight)
- rolling the cloth in plastic will prevent it drying out too much and protect your surfaces if curing and batching inside the house. Rolling is better than folding as sometimes, crease marks can set into the cloth. If you don't want to roll, then let the cloth get almost dry, and scrumple it into a plastic bag for batching
- if you want a blurred output, the cloth can be rolled in plastic whilst still very wet
- if you want to keep the crisp marks and delicate impressions, let the printed cloth get almost dry before rolling in plastic.

Once cured, you can rinse your cloth.

Writing, Doodles & Squiggles

So far, so great! The next variation is to write, doodle, squirt and make squiggle marks using the thick dye paint(s) on the back of the screen. This can be done as a second layer on top of a first layer of dried-on dye colour(s), or as a single layer, leaving gaps between the lines/marks.

Applying The Dyes

We find a squeeze bottle is the best application method. As the dye paint is thicker than normal, take it slowly as squeezing will be quite hard on the hands. Experimentation is the way forward here, and about the only general advice we can give is...

- Lay down your screen(s) with the back (print) side up and create a well using masking tape if you wish to.
- Assemble your colour range in squeeze bottles.
- Work in close colours, monochromatically, or in a variety of colours.
- Hold the bottle nozzle down, squeeze and write, doodle or squiggle.
- The faster you move the bottle, the thinner the lines.
- If you want clear, identifiable lines, make sure there's a reasonable gap between the lines as the dye paint will settle and spread a little. Make sure the screen is kept flat, and left to dry flat.
- If you want the marks/lines to mingle and form an eventual solid layer of different colours, or have very slight gaps between the lines, go crazy with the bottle(s) and tilt the screen for a while to encourage inter-mingling before leaving it flat to dry.
- Either way, expect some of the dye paint to seep through and drip off whilst the screen is lying flat to dry. Consider putting a piece of dry, soda-soaked cloth under the screen to catch the drips in order to start a new, random piece of work.

Whichever approach you take, leave the screen flat to let the applied dye(s) dry out completely.

Using print paste and dye paint to print

The print paste and dye paint mixture can create streaky effects when 'mixed' through the well/screen

The dried-on dye doodle marks print in the negative image

The dried-on dye doodle releases itself, breakdown is happening

Printing Off

If you've 'gone crazy' and have an almost solid surface of colour, consider beginning your printing in the same manner as 'Making an Impression'; use clear print paste. The process will be very similar to printing off the 'Impression' screens and you can switch to using a full or weakened dye colour as you progress.

If you created lines/doodles/squiggles/writing with clear gaps in between, use full strength or weakened dye paints rather than clear print paste (as outlined under 'Making an Impression'). Why? If you start with clear print paste, the gaps in between the dye doodles will only be of the very palest tint as it'll take longer than usual for the dye-on-screen to tint the paste, as there's less of it.

Remember, when choosing your dye colours, work to avoid mud (unless that's what you want)!

To begin with, the thick lines of dye-on-screen will act as a resist, leaving you with a white/pale outline of your doodle, surrounded by whatever colour of dye paint you're using to print off with – in other words, a negative image. As the dye-on-screen gets wetter, it will gradually dissolve and start to release, printing itself as a rough positive image until there's nothing left on the screen.

So, as with 'Making an Impression', you can explore the following options;

- mix 'n match with new colours – just be aware of the possibility for mud!
- over-print; again, be aware of what's happening as you work. Be careful not to over saturate the cloth with heavy over-printing as you may obscure some of your original prints, or they may get too wet and bleed and blur out.

Now cure/batch your cloth and then rinse as before.

Tilting the screen to encourage runs, sags and bags

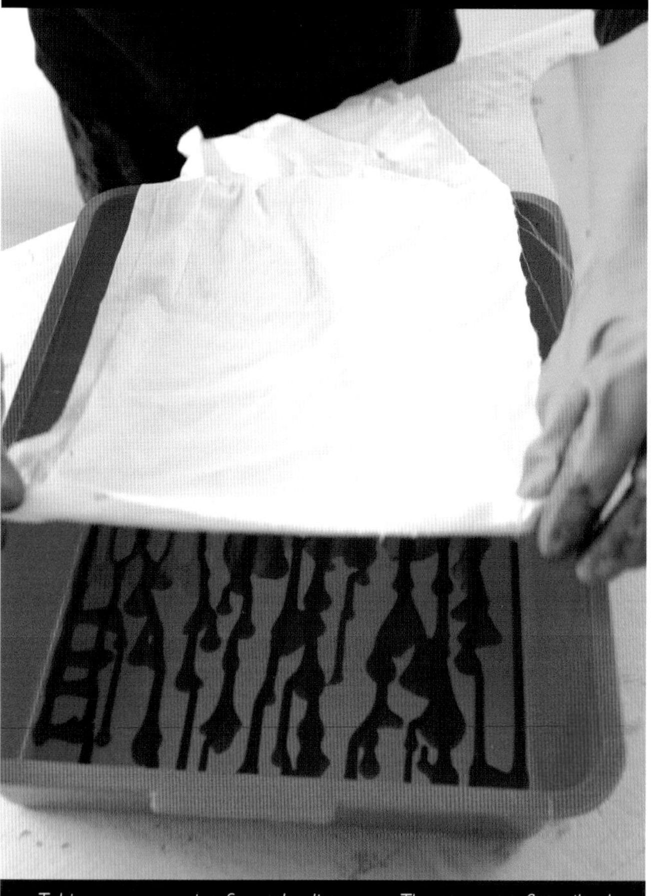

Taking a monoprint from the litter tray. The tray was first tilted to let the drips of dye run down the tray

Runs & Drips

The next variation is to deliberately create runs, sags, bags and drips on the screen. It's slightly wasteful of dyes, but we'll show you a way of using the leftovers that's great for embroiderers or quilt-makers (who piece) as it uses small pieces of cloth.

Begin by assembling your colour palette of thick dyes, a cat litter tray and your screens (create a well on them using torn or straight-edge masking tape if you want to).

Applying the Dyes

Apply the dyes using foam brushes as you would when 'Making an Impression'. Keep the screen flat, paint up sections of close or varying colours, or cover it in a single colour. Next...

- Stand the screen upright or at an angle in a cat litter/seed tray or on plastic and squirt on extra blobs of dye (similar or different colours) and let them run, sag and bag until you're happy with the results. As soon as you're happy, lay the screen flat (painted side up) on top of the tray/plastic.
- The dyes will begin to drip through and out of the other side – the tray/plastic will catch the excess.
- Let the screen dry thoroughly.
- Once the screen is dry, take it away from the tray/plastic, which will be spotted with dye. At this stage, you can lay a piece of damp or dry soda-soaked cloth in the tray to pick up the drips (or you could lay this down from the very beginning). Alternatively, tilt the tray/plastic and let this excess dye run; wiggle and tilt to create patterns and lines and then lay down a piece of dry soda-soaked cloth – essentially you're making a mono-print. Let the cloth dry off a bit (or not as the case may be) and cure/batch and rinse it in the normal way – an extra piece of cloth for further exploration.

Now, back to the dried screen(s).

Printing with dye that has been pre-mixed with print paste to dilute the value

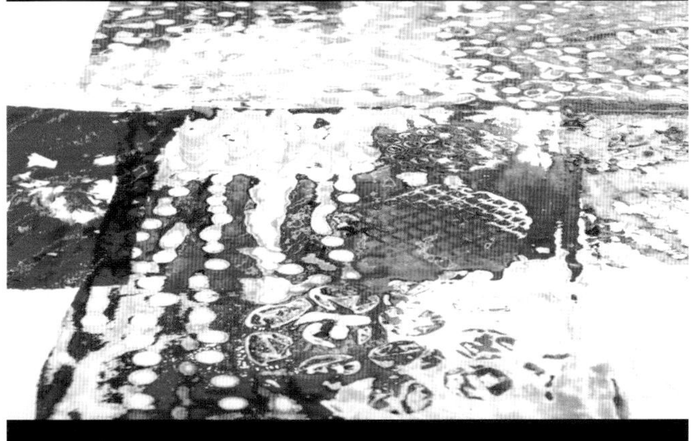

The organic quality of drips and runs printed in negative image

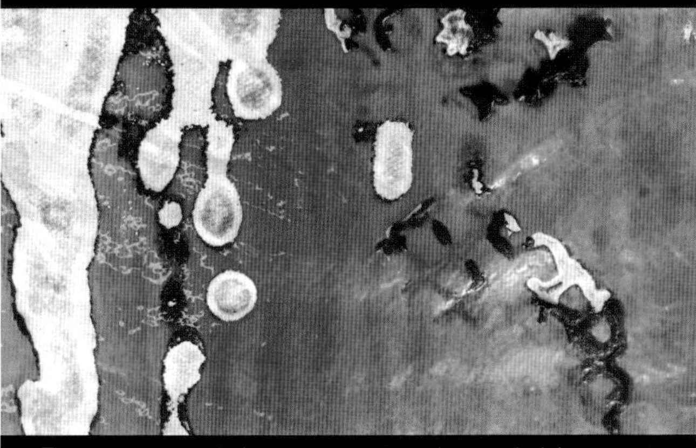

The negative marks/images sometimes have a 'halo' of colour around them

Printing up a large piece of cloth

Printing Off

Pin out your dry, soda-soaked cloth on to the bench and gather together the things you'll need;

- clear print paste in a pot with a spoon, or in a squeeze bottle
- a range of dye colours in full or weaker strengths
- a squeegee
- a cat litter tray
- rubber gloves

As with 'Making an Impression' this approach generally starts with the use of clear print paste as the media, but you can also start with full or weakened dyes.

- Place down the screen (flat/painted side down) – avoiding dead-centre or extreme edge placement.
- Spoon or squirt some clear print paste/dye into the top or right-hand side of the screen.
- Pull! Again, it's hard to say how many pulls will start to release the dye-on-screen, so anchor and tilt the screen after about three pulls and take a peek.
- Move the screen to another part of the cloth and make another print. Continue in this manner and expect to see (roughly!) the following;

- thinner layers of dye will be used up faster than thicker areas - the sag/bag/drip areas are likely to be acting as a resist, or laying down very uneven areas of colour as they resist print-off.
- these run/sag/bag/drip areas may simply print a halo at the extreme edges
- points where the dye has dripped through the screen before drying off may print as 'cigarette burns' (thanks for this description Rita!)
- ultimately, where areas of dye paint print off faster than others, the voids will get tinted with a pale wash of colour from the print paste, or the dye colour you're using.

- Once again, if you've started with clear print paste, you can choose to switch to using full strength or weakened dye paints at any stage and you can introduce new colours at any point – just as you did when printing off 'Making an Impression'.

Be aware of what's happening as you work. Be careful not to over saturate the cloth with heavy handed over-printing as some of the fine, delicate textural marks made by the runs, sags, bags and drips may get too wet and bleed and blur out as discussed earlier – not necessarily a disaster and perhaps just what you want – just be aware of what's happening as you work.

When you're done, let the printed cloth dry off a bit, then cure/batch and rinse in the normal way.

Doodling on a layer of dried dye

Combining breakdown approaches on a single screen

Printing with two different breakdown screens

Printing with two colours at once (magenta & turquoise)

Variations on a Theme

The potential of breakdown printing is unlimited as long as you keep asking 'what if?'. Once you've got the basic principles, you can experiment endlessly but rather than repeat ourselves in terms of process instructions, here are some further variations to get your curiosity going…

• Combine approaches;

- coat the screen with a single layer of dye and let it dry. Then write, doodle or squiggle on top of the dried-on dye and let it dry off again.
- make a screen with 'Impressions', then apply the 'Runs & Drips' approach to some areas. If you do this, make sure your extra squirts of dye to create runs aren't directly above something you've applied for an Impression – when you tilt the screen the running dye may well push applied items down and off the screen
- use the 'Writing, Doodles & Squiggles' approach, then tilt the screen to make it run and blend.

• Make one of each type of screen; an Impression, a Doodle and a Run & Drip. Use all three on one piece of cloth.

• Print on white, pre-dyed or pre-printed cloth.

• Print with one prepared screen only, or two, or six.

• Print off sections of the screen, rather than all of the screen.

• Leave prints independent of each other, or over-print.

• Print with a prepared screen, and use a blank screen to over-print or lay down solid'ish areas of colour.

• Print using two colours in the screen at once.

Keep asking 'what if' and you'll expand this list considerably.

Spreading print paste on to a blank screen

Making an impression into the spread print paste using rubber mesh & bubble wrap

Doodles marks using print paste

First print of a print-paste doodle screen using dye paint

Print Paste for Discharge & Dye Work
Instead of using thick dye paints, you can apply clear print paste on screen in the same manner;

Making Impressions with Print Paste; apply the print paste all over the back of the screen using a foam brush. Try to make the depth of coverage uneven as this will give you more interesting results. Apply the items you wish to make an impression with and leave the screen to dry flat, just as you did when using dye paints.

Drips & Runs; this will be successful if you ensure that you generate a combination of thin and thick areas of print paste. We often combine 'Impressions' with 'Drips and Runs'.

Writing, Doodles & Squiggles; as the print paste is colourless, there's little point in allowing your doodling to blend and mingle in the same way as you might with a range of dye colours. So, doodle to allow blank, clear spaces and remember that the applied print paste will act as a chemical resist, so when you come to print with dyes or discharge paste, you'll print the blanks – a negative image.

You can now print using thick dye paints or discharge agents, let's look at these options independently.

Print-Off using Thick Dye Paint
Pin out your soda-soaked and dried cloth on to the bench and gather together the things you'll need;

- thick dye paints in colour(s) and strengths of your choice
- a squeegee
- a cat litter tray
- rubber gloves

Essentially, you'll print off in the same manner as you would if you'd painted the screen with dyes, but you'll start by using dye paints as your media rather than clear print paste. As such, this approach works well with the 'Writing, Doodles & Squiggles' approach where you've left good voids. The doodle design in applied print paste will act as a resist and you'll print the void as a negative image in dye.

The dried on-screen print paste will dilute the dye strengths a little as you progress. This will give you variations in depth and colour according to the different amounts/thicknesses of the paste on-screen, how quickly it breaks down and so on. Keep printing until the screen has broken down to the point that you choose to stop using it.

Let your cloth dry off a little, then batch and rinse as usual.

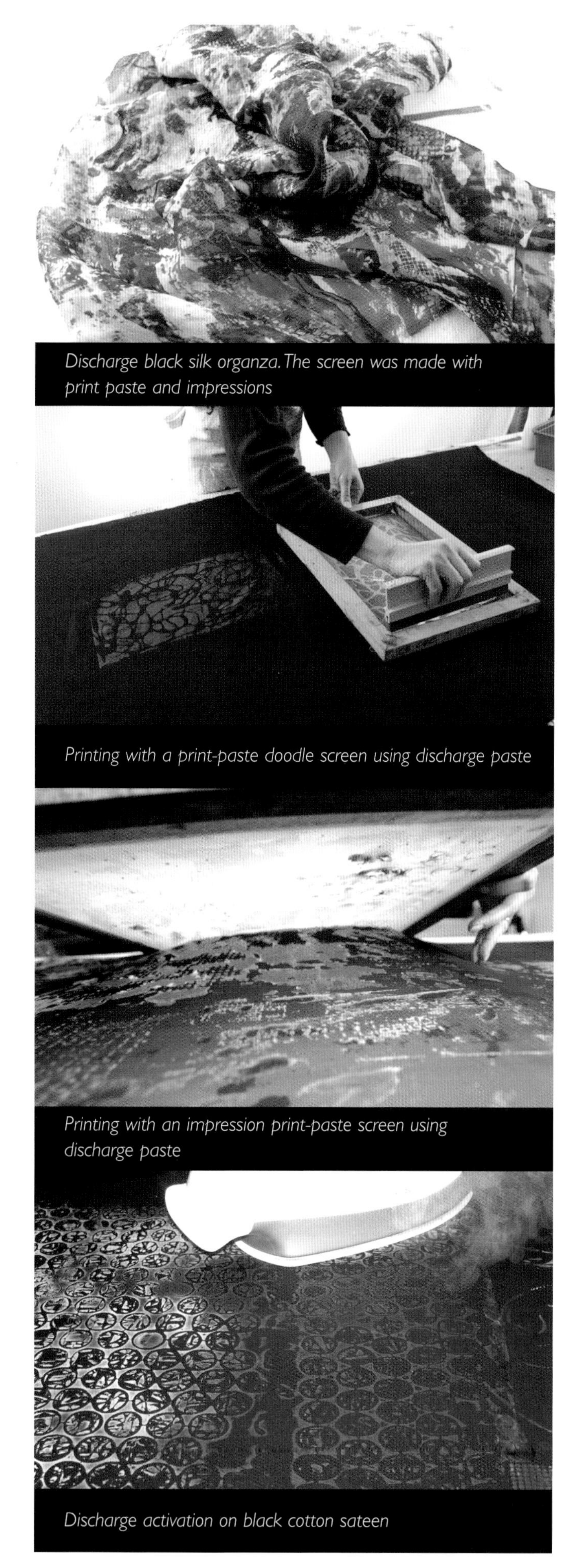

Discharge black silk organza. The screen was made with print paste and impressions

Printing with a print-paste doodle screen using discharge paste

Printing with an impression print-paste screen using discharge paste

Discharge activation on black cotton sateen

Print-Off using Discharge Media

You can use prepared print-paste screens with commercially produced discharge agents. Discharge is the term used for the process of removing colour from pre-dyed cloth. We use Jacquard Discharge paste which is suitable for cotton, linen, viscose (rayon) and silk. The active ingredient is triggered by a combination of heat and steam so once the paste has been applied, the cloth needs to be steam-ironed on the cotton setting.

You'll need pre-dyed cloth of a medium-to-dark value. This could be;

- *Hand-dyes*; all Procion Mx dyes will discharge but beware Turquoise; it can be very stubborn and often refuses to discharge at all with Discharge Paste. Otherwise, most hand-dyes will discharge. The more colour present in the cloth (both in terms of range and depth of colour), the more varied the results. So, choose a pre-dyed piece in a plain/solid colour, a piece that's been dyed with multiple colours or a piece that you've printed with the breakdown method.
- *Commercially dyed*; some commercially dyed cloth may not discharge at all, or the discharged result could be very unpredictable, so test a small piece first.
- *Commercial discharge cloth*; cloth that's been commercially prepared for discharge will generate excellent results.

Important note; if you're going to print using discharge paste don't soda soak your cloth, but do scour it first to remove size.

Make sure the cloth is dry, pin it out and assemble;

- Your prepared and dried screen(s)
- a squeegee
- discharge paste
- spoon
- cat litter tray
- rubber gloves
- a steam iron
- a mask (or work outside/in a well-ventilated area).

Printing with Discharge Paste

- Place your prepared and dried screen flat/painted side down – avoiding dead-centre or extreme edge placement.
- Place your squeegee (in the well if you've created one) at the top end or right-hand side of the screen and spoon or squirt a bead of discharge paste in front of it.
- Pull away – again, it's hard to say how many pulls will enable the paste to get through the dried-on print paste as it depends how it's been applied, so anchor and tilt the screen after about 3 and take a peek. If not much media has come through, do more pulls.
- Move the screen to another part of the cloth and make another print. Make 3 to 4 prints, then scoop out the excess discharge paste and deposit it into a cat litter tray, along with your squeegee. Lean the screen against the table as it's time to activate the discharge paste.

Discharge activation on black silk organza

Discharge beginning to happen on previously dyed and printed cloth

Detail of breakdown discharge printing on black cotton sateen

Discharge Activation

Discharge Paste is best activated damp – regardless of the instructions you read on the jar! Activation happens through a combination of heat and steam, so you'll need to steam iron your prints. This creates fumes so do this in a well ventilated environment and ideally, wear a good mask.

As the prints will be damp, don't iron in the normal manner as this will drag and smear the wet paste across the cloth. Instead, lift the iron up and down on to the cloth using a patting motion. Stay in the same general area for some time, as the damp paste takes a while to activate. You'll gradually see your cloth change colour – to what is hard to say as this depends on the colours present in the cloth to begin with.

Once the paste has begun to dry out, you can switch to ironing in the normal way… and do keep going, as there's often more discharge potential left than you think. On the other hand, if you like what you see then stop ironing; the process is fairly controllable.

Having discharged your first set of prints, print 3 to 4 more, activate the paste with the screen iron, then print 3 to 4 more and activate again. Continue in this manner until the screen is no longer of any use as the design has broken down.

It's then important to rinse the cloth. It will be holding a residue of dried-in discharge paste and print paste that needs to be washed away. A warm hand or machine wash with a drop of rinsing agent will do it. Dry the cloth and admire your results!

Clean Up

Dye paints and discharge media will wash out of your screen, tools and implements with cold or warm water.

Screens; wash out screens under running water. Use a brush and really get into the corners and the edge where the mesh meets the frame. Do a thorough job. Dry off with an old towel to get rid of excess water and make sure the mesh is dry before you use the screen again. Avoid drying screens in strong sunlight or over direct heat. Store screens in an upright position away from sharp objects and direct heat/sunlight. Don't stack screens as this may cause warping.

Squeegees; wash under cold running water using a brush. Go at the squeegee – it'll take a good few minutes to truly get rid of dye that's crept up the blade and into the handle. Drain by standing on end so that any excess media left behind drains out, or towel dry if you're in a hurry to use it again.

Other tools; litter trays, spoons, bottles, foam brushes etc. can all be washed under running cold water. Stack to dry or towel dry.

Cleaning the screen

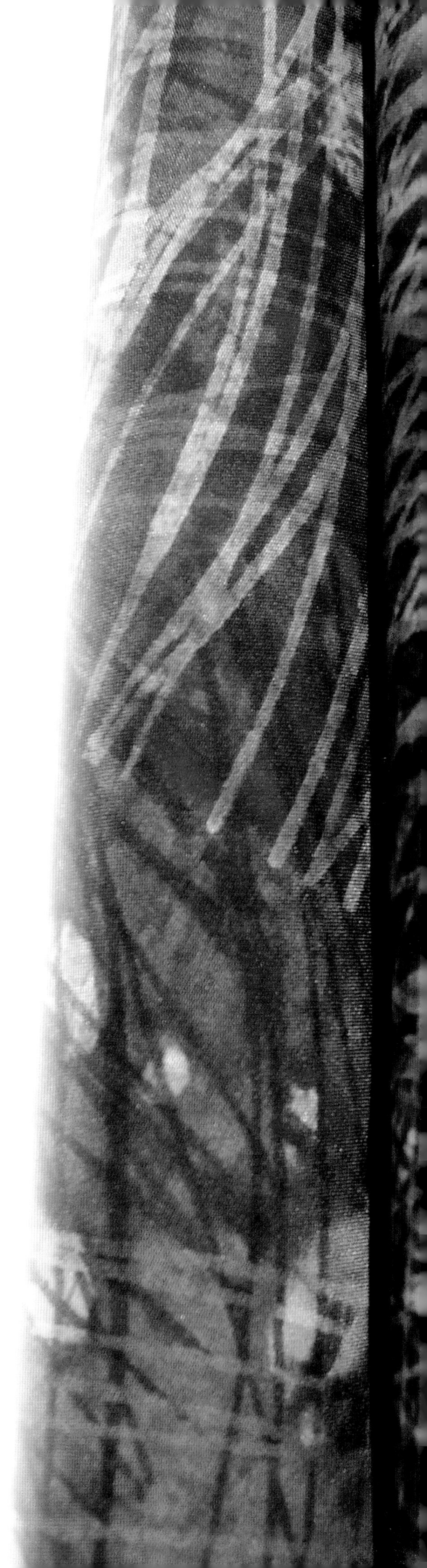

Left: A selection of over-dyed 'breakdown' cloth

More black cotton sateen. Breakdown printed, hand-printed with letter forms (screen inks) then printed with gold leaf. Work in progress.

Curing/Batching & Rinsing the Cloth

Curing / Batching

The cloth that you've printed with dye paints will need to cure or batch in order to fix the dyes. Three conditions are required to maximise the dye/fibre reaction:

Moisture: almost dry to the touch or very wet
Heat: 15°C - 35°C (60°F - 85°F)
Time: 4 - 24 hours (4 is the absolute minimum)

Moisture

Dye molecules can penetrate the fibre of the cloth more effectively when moisture is present, although the amount of moisture can be so little that the fabric can feel almost dry to the touch. If the fabric becomes bone dry, the reaction may stop completely, so avoid drying your freshly printed cloth in direct sunlight as this may cause the dye paint to dry out too quickly, resulting in poor colour strike/faded colours as the batching time is reduced. If your printed cloth does seem to have dried out completely, decant some of your soda stock into a plant mister and spray the dried-out cloth very lightly with the soda solution. Then roll or cover it with plastic.

The best way to retain enough moisture content is to use plastic sheeting – either leave the cloth on the bench and cover it with plastic, or roll it up into plastic. Try to avoid folding pieces (in or out of its rolled plastic) as crease marks can sometimes set permanently. As the Breakdown process creates fairly organic cloth in style, another option is to simply crumple the cloth up into a plastic bag once it's almost dry.

Rolling the almost-dry printed cloth into plastic

Rolling the cloth up when very wet may cause colours to bleed and blend, which can be fantastic. If you want to keep colours separate, or keep very crisp marks and lines, don't cover or roll when very wet - let the cloth get almost dry (on the bench or on the line) then cover or roll in plastic and cure.

Heat

Cure between 15°C - 35°C (60°F - 85°F). If the temperature's too cold, the reaction of the dye is slowed down or even halted completely. To hot and it may dry too quickly for proper curing.

In the summer, or if the studio is heated overnight, let the printed cloth sit overnight, curing gradually in or under plastic. In winter or in an un-heated studio, roll it up in plastic sheeting (very wet or almost-dry) and bring it into the house and place somewhere warm; under (but not on top of) a radiator or in an airing cupboard. We use a folded-over electric blanket as a 'hot box', sliding the tubes of rolled up plastic between the layers. The blanket provides even background heat at very little cost.

Time

Allow between 4 and 24 hours for curing as the dye needs time to react with the fibre molecules. 4 hours is an absolute minimum - our normal curing time is 12-18 hours/overnight for most applications to extract a good reaction/dye take-up.

Rinsing

If you can use Synthrapol/Metapex 38, so much the better, as it will "trap" dye particles and prevent colour contamination. If you do use Synthrapol/Metapex 38, you'll need a few drops when hand-rinsing, and about a half teaspoon when machine washing, depending on the size of the load and the heaviness of the fibre. If you don't have Synthrapol, use a mild detergent, such as you might use for washing fine woollens.

- Rinse off excess dye in cold water and Synthrapol/detergent, using a bucket in the sink and changing the water regularly.
- Machine wash cold with Synthrapol, once or possibly twice
- Machine wash again in warm water with Synthrapol (30-40°C)

If you wash in hot water too quickly, excess dye particles may transfer and cause back and cross staining (although the use of Synthrapol will help to prevent this). Remember, the stronger the colours/the more dye you've used, the more washes you'll need. If you know you're taking the cloth on to another dye or say, discharge process that will subsequently entail more washing, just hand-rinse cold, machine rinse cold and then carry on with the next wet process.

The Breakdown process uses thicker than usual dye paints and the Manutex in the dye paints/print paste can often prove to be stubborn – you'll know if this has happened as the cloth will still feel stiff after rinsing and drying. If you find the Manutex is behaving stubbornly, do a hot soda soak/rinse after the initial cold rinsing;

- dissolve 1-3 tablespoons of soda in hot (but not boiling) water. The amount of soda is dependent on the size of the piece of cloth
- add a drop of Synthrapol/Metapex 38
- give the piece a good mashing in the bucket, then leave to soak for 10-30 minutes, mashing from time to time
- rinse out by hand in warm to hot water
- do a final warm water rinse by machine.

If the Manutex still hasn't shifted, repeat the process.

higher
a far

Re-working a piece of breakdown-printed cloth using a squiggle

Over-printing using a variety of breakdown screens and a blank screen

Additional printing with dye paints. A sticky-back stencil is on the back of the screen

Printing on breakdown cloth using traditional letter forms and black screen ink

Building on the Cloth

As discussed in the introduction, creating fabulous cloth with that 'Complex Cloth' look generally doesn't happen with a single process. Occasionally it does, but don't expect it. So, consider building up layers of process on your cloth by using a combination of the following approaches – and Jane Dunnewold's book, Complex Cloth (Fiber Studio Press, 1996) – will given you even more ideas.

- Re-print with different 'Breakdown' dye-on-screen approaches; soda soak and dry your printed cloth. Prepare a new Breakdown screen and re-print with it.

- Re-print with different 'Breakdown' paste-on-screen approaches; soda soak and dry your printed cloth. Prepare a new Breakdown screen with clear print paste and print it off with dye paints.

- Discharge using 'Breakdown' paste-on-screen; use a newly prepared screen and this time, use discharge paste as the print media (do not soda soak the cloth for discharge applications).

- Re-print with a blank screen; soda-soak and dry your printed cloth and then lay down colour washes by printing with thick dye paints through a blank screen.

- Re-printing with additional imagery; soda-soak and dry your printed cloth, then create imagery on the screen by using sticky-back plastic or torn/cut masking tape. Jane Dunnewold's book 'Improvisational Screen Printing' will give you many alternative ways to create imagery using a screen. Print with dyes, discharge paste or textile paints/screen inks.

- Over-dyeing; you could choose to over-dye your printed cloth. If so, be careful with the dye strength as you might obliterate what you've got (see illustration on page 24).

- Direct surface applications; mix some dye paints to any consistency you want using Thin Chemical Water, Thick Print Paste or a combination thereof to get what you want (see the 'Recipes' section at the back). Spray it on to your printed cloth, or paint it, throw it, spatter it, drag it, stipple it, stamp it and so forth.

- And lets not forget dry processes; cutting and piecing, stitching, embroidery, appliqué and so forth.

How you use your 'Breakdown' printed cloth is up to you...

- Stitched textiles
- Quilts
- Embroidery
- Clothing
- Accessories such as scarves and bags
- Soft furnishings such as cushions and blinds
- Book covers

Or just stroke it and enjoy it.

Recipes

The following recipes aren't definitive - every book you read will have a different variation. This is not to say that some are better than others, they're just different and reflect the preferences of the individual artist/author.

Soda-Soaking
Remember to Soda-soak your fabric in advance. Use the table below as a guide for mixing your soda solution.

Meterage	Water	Soda Ash
2-3 metres	2 litres	90ml / 5 tbsp
4-6 metres	4 litres	180ml / 10tbsp
6-8 metres	6 litres	270ml / 15 tbsp
8-10 metres	8 litres	360ml / 20 tbsp
10-14 metres	10 litres	450ml / 25 tbsp

Thin Chemical Water

- Thin Chemical Water is the starting point for all dye paints. Dye is added to it to create a mixture that's suitable for spraying, painting or spattering.

- You can use thin chemical water containing Urea, Calgon and Ludigol/Resist Salt L, or a simplified version that simply uses Urea (the hydroscopic agent that keeps the dye paint from drying out too quickly). However, if you live in a hard water area, do use a water softener such as Calgon otherwise your dye strike may be weaker. Ludigol/Resist Salt L is an anti-oxidant and useful where air pollution may distort the dye colours. Either way, it's still Chemical Water, and it can be convenient to have it ready to hand. Stored cool, it will keep indefinitely and volume quantities are:

Warm Water	Urea	Ludigol	Calgon
1/2 litre (500ml)	100ml / 70g	2.5ml	2.5ml
1 litre	200ml / 160g	5ml	5ml
5 litres	500ml / 400g	25ml	25ml
10 litres	1000ml / 800g	50ml	50ml

As a rough guide, 50ml urea = 35g weighed.

In hot weather, increase the quantity of Urea by approximately 10-20% to prevent the dye paints from drying out too quickly.

Thick Print Paste

- A thickening agent (Sodium Alginate/Manutex RS) is added to the Thin Chemical Water to create Thick Chemical Paste or 'Print Paste'. Dye is dissolved in a little warm water and then the Print Paste is added to the mixture to create a consistency of dye paint suitable for screen printing or stamping.

- We usually make about 4 litres of Print Paste at a time and keep it in the fridge, where it will last for 4-6 weeks. If you've got some that's been hanging around for longer than this, it may smell of ammonia and have gone off. Dyes can still strike in old paste but the colour can be less intense, so if you want to be sure, mix a new batch.

- *The quantity of Manutex RS/alginate used in the following recipe will make a thicker-than-usual paste which is perfect for Breakdown screen printing.* A normal/thinner consistency of print paste isn't suitable as too much drips through the screen as it dries, and breakdown occurs too rapidly.

Thin Chemical Water	Sodium Alginate/Manutex
1 litre	45ml / 35g
2 litres	90ml / 70-75g
4 litres	190ml / 130g

- To mix, pour your chosen amount of thin chemical water into a plastic container and sprinkle on the Manutex RS/alginate, stirring as you do so. Use of a hand-held electric mixer will make blending easy, but thorough stirring will get good results. Once mixed, the paste will initially still be quite runny and must be left (covered) in a cool place for at least 4 hours to thicken up, ideally overnight. If mixing by hand as opposed to using a mixer, it can be a good idea to stir the paste again after a couple of hours to break up any lumps.

- If you wish to reduce the thickness of the paste, it can be thinned down for normal screen printing and other direct surface applications by adding a little more thin chemical water.

Thick Dye Paints

How much dye you put into your paint mixture is dependent on you – the more dye, the more intense the colour. Equally, the type of fabric you're using will determine the colour strength.

A good starting point is to mix up a medium-to-dark mixture (e.g. 4tsp to 500ml) and reduce the colour value by adding more print paste if you need to. We don't attempt precise measurements and the table represents a rough guide when mixing half-litres (500ml) of any consistency paint.

Always mix dyes in a small amount of warm-to-hot water until dissolved, and then top up to 500ml with print paste. If making smaller quantities, alter the amounts proportionately.

Per 500ml Print Paste	Dye Qty
Pale-to-Medium	1/8 - 1 teaspoon
Medium-to-Dark	1 - 4 teaspoons
Dark-to-Very Dark	4 - 6 teaspoons

Striking; generally speaking, yellows and reds (and therefore oranges) strike more effectively than blues and blacks.
Black; when mixing black, you may want to consider doubling the dye quantity to get a true black.
Turquoise; blues and blacks generally strike less than yellows, reds or oranges and Turquoise can sometimes be a little feeble, so consider increasing the quantity of Turquoise by half.
Yellow; when mixing yellow, consider increasing the quantities by half as whilst it strikes well, yellow is easily bullied out/contaminated by other colours.

Ultimately, the results depend on dye paint strengths, fibre types, curing/fixing time and curing temperature (warmer is better). Colour take-up is generally stronger on silk than on cotton. The silk fibres are finer and therefore more easily saturated with colour. If you're using cotton, consider increasing the dye quantities given here by 50% or be prepared to repeat the Breakdown process.

You'll need to experiment and/or undertake samples. The more you do, the more you practice, the more you'll engage with the process and understand it. Ultimately, you'll establish what dye strength is needed to achieve the result you're looking for on the cloth you're using.

Procion Mx dyes will gradually bond with water at warmer temperatures, so their shelf life is limited once mixed. Shelf life can be prolonged by keeping the mixtures in the fridge (covered), but it can be risky to use them after 4 weeks and there's no guarantee on results. We have risked using paints that are 6 months old, but the colours were very pale.

Other Dye-Paint Consistencies

Using Thin Chemical Water instead of Print Paste will create a paint mixture that's suitable for other direct surface applications such as watercolour washes, spraying, spattering etc. To mix, pour a small amount of warm water into a wide-mouthed beaker, add your dye and mix thoroughly into a runny paste, and then gradually top up with Chemical Water. Stir or shake well to get rid of any lumps.

Equally, you can make any consistency between thin and thick, by mixing thin chemical water with thick print paste to get what you want.

Resources/Suppliers

Our website (www.committedtocloth.com) has a list of suppliers, but those shown below will be able to supply you with the tools and media required for Breakdown printing. They are listed in alphabetical order and we have given an indication of what they can provide you.

Art Van Go
The Studios, 1 Stevenage Road, Knebworth, Herts G3 6AN
Telephone: 01438 814946
www.artvango.co.uk

Shop, van and mail-order. Very helpful. AvG can supply cloth, dyes, textile paints, discharge paste, screens, squeegees, chemicals (Urea etc.) tools and a huge variety of art and craft materials and items.

Fibrecrafts/George Weil
Old Portsmouth Road, Peasmarsh, Guildford, Surrey GU3 1LZ
Telephone: 01483 565800
www.fibrecrafts.co.uk

Shop and mail order. Fibrecrafts can supply cloth, dyes, textile paints, discharge media, chemicals (Urea etc.) screens, squeegees, screen mesh and a large variety of fibre-related products and supplies.

Kemtex Educational Supplies
Chorley Business & Technology Centre, Euxton Lane,
Chorley, Lancs PR7 6TE
Telephone: 01257 230220
www.kemtex.co.uk

Bulk/volume supplies, although some items such as dyes are available from 100gm upwards. Dyes, chemicals such as Urea, Soda Ash, Ludigol/Resist Salt L, Manutex RS/Sodium Alginate etc. Kemtex do not sell cloth or tools such as screens.

Patchwork Shop
Web; www.patchworkshop.de or www.pdpm.de

Based in Germany, this is an excellent outlet. Whilst much of the on-line shop is in German, the pictures are clear and Guenther speaks excellent English – so just email him with your requirements and he'll sort you out. They stock an excellent range of PDF (prepared for dyeing) cloth. The cotton sateen No's 3 and 11 are gorgeous, as is the black discharge cotton sateen. 150cm wide acrylic felt (for print boards), dyes, Deka Textile Paints, Discharge Paste, screens, screen mesh, a wide variety of squeegees, chemicals, squeeze bottles etc. etc. Guenther also provides a mail order thermo-screen service.

Rainbow Silks
6 Wheelers Yard, High Street, Great Missenden, Bucks HP16 0AL
Telephone: 01494 862111

Mail order and shop. Some cloth, embroidery supplies, textile paints & dyes (small pots, usually 50ml) and tools.

Whaleys
Harris Court, Great Horton, Bradford, West Yorkshire
Telephone: 01274 57678
www.whaleys-bradford.ltd.uk

Mail order. An enormous range of cloth, with many prepared for dyeing (PDF). Ring and ask for a brochure. Sample book available to purchase and samples sent on request.

Winifred Cottage
17 Elms Road, Fleet, Hampshire GU51 3EG
Telephone: 01252 617667
Email: WinifCott@aol.com

Embroidery supplies, hand-dyes and commercial threads, needles, 150cm wide acrylic felt (for covering print boards) and much, much more.

Wolfin Textiles
359 Uxbridge Road, Hatch End, Middlesex HA5 4JN
Telephone: 020 8428 9911
www.wolfintextiles.co.uk

Basic cottons and linens, plus odd-balls such as Nun's veiling!

Other suppliers outside of Europe that are worth exploring include;

Dick Blick
PO Box 1267, Galesburgh, IL 61402, U.S.A.
www.dickblick.com

A huge arts and crafts mail order company. Look at the website and drool.

ProChemical & Dye
PO Box 14, Somerset, MA 02726, U.S.A.
www.prochemical.com

Fantastic selection of dyes, paints, chemicals, tools and related products.

Rupert, Gibbon & Spider, Inc
PO Box 452, Healdsburg, CA 95448, U.S.A.

Manufacturers of Jacquard dyes, discharge paste, textile paints and other media. Great selection of cloth.

Tip;
Certain supplies can be bought very cheaply…
Soda Ash; can be purchased in bulk (5kg containers +) from swimming pool supply companies. Ask for Alkali ph Plus and check that it's a pure soda ash and not had chlorine added to it.
Urea; can be bought from animal feed merchants, although you'll need to buy 25kg at a time!